Environmental Time Bomb

Other titles in the Issues in Focus *series:*

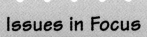

Issues in Focus

Environmental Time Bomb

Our Threatened Planet

Patricia Haddock

Enslow Publishers, Inc.

40 Industrial Road   PO Box 38
Box 398   Aldershot
Berkeley Heights, NJ 07922   Hants GU12 6BP
USA   UK

http://www.enslow.com

Library of Congress Cataloging-in-Publication Data

Haddock, Patricia.
    Environmental time bomb : our threatened planet / by Patricia
Haddock.
        p. cm. — (Issues in focus)
    Includes bibliographical references and index.
    Summary: Examines a wide range of environmental problems
including overpopulation, biodiversity, pollution, and
conservation and encourages readers to become involved in trying
to solve these problems.
    ISBN 0-7660-1229-8
    1. Environmental quality—Juvenile literature. [1. Environmental
protection. 2. Conservation of natural resources.] I. Title. II. Issues
in focus (Hillside, N.J.)
GE140.5 .H33   2000
363.7—dc21
                                99-050938

Printed in the United States of America

10 9 8 7 6 5 4 3 2 1

To Our Readers:
All Internet addresses in this book were active and appropriate when we
went to press. Any comments or suggestions can be sent by e-mail to
Comments@enslow.com or to the address on the back cover.

Every effort has been made to locate all copyright holders of material
used in this book. If any errors or omissions have occurred, corrections
will be made in future editions of this book.

Illustration Credits: Corel, pp. 10, 32, 40; Department of
Energy, p. 27; National Archives and Records Administration,
pp. 19, 21, 37, 50, 60, 63, 74, 77, 80, 83, 87; National
Oceanographic and Atmospheric Agency (NOAA), p. 69; NOAA
Brooke Vallaster, p. 97; NOAA Commander John Bortniak (ret),
pp. 65, 72; NOAA Mary Hollinger, p. 52; NOAA National
Marine Fisheries Service, p. 90; NOAA OAR/National Undersea
Research Program, p. 87; NOAA Personnel of PIERCE, p. 44;
United Nations, p. 57; United States Fish and Wildlife Service,
pp. 14, 93.

Cover Illustration: National Archives and Records Administration

Contents

1

"Going Green": The Environmental Movement

On March 23, 1989, in the middle of the night, one of the most beautiful and pristine places in the world was fouled by one of the worst environmental disasters in history. The *Exxon Valdez* oil tanker, which was traveling through Prince William Sound in Alaska, hit a reef. The impact gouged holes in the ship and 41.6 million liters (11 million gallons) of crude oil spilled into the water.

Prince William Sound had been a haven for a rich variety of wildlife, including endangered and threatened species. Thousands of people depended on the

Sound for food, and many worked there in the fishing and tourism industries.

According to government estimates, the oil spill killed as many as 250 bald eagles, 2,800 sea otters, and more than 200,000 sea birds. In addition, the harvest of pink salmon was canceled that year, harming the economy of dozens of small towns that relied on the catch for their livelihood.

Hundreds of planes, 1,000 ships, and more than 11,000 workers were needed to help clean up the spill. Workers scrubbed beaches and rocks for three years. They cleaned and treated sick sea otters and bald eagles at a cost of $80,000 per saved otter and $10,000 per eagle. The Exxon Corporation's cost for the clean-up alone was more than $2 billion. This does not even include financial settlements from lawsuits and fines leveled by the federal government.[1]

The *Exxon Valdez* oil spill occurred more than ten years ago. Since then, Prince William Sound has made a miraculous comeback and we have learned a lot about how to prevent and clean up oil spills.

While oil spills are often large-scale, dramatic environmental disasters that get lots of news coverage, they are not the only environmental problems. The world faces a multitude of environmental challenges, each with a variety of possible solutions. Each solution has an impact that can be positive or negative depending on your point of view.

The Beginnings of the Modern Environmental Movement

The modern environmental movement began in Maine in the early 1960s. Rachel Carson's neighbor mentioned to her that she never saw robins on her lawn anymore. Carson, a well-known author and scientist, was intrigued and started to do some research on the missing birds. In 1962, Carson published *Silent Spring*, an account of the chain of effects the pesticide DDT had on the environment. Carson's book was an eye-opener. She warned of the fragility of nature and the dangers of releasing chemicals into the environment—especially those that, like DDT, might cause cancer. A sad irony was that just two years after *Silent Spring* was published, Carson died of cancer.

Silent Spring caught the attention of President John F. Kennedy. His interest helped spark public concern about a range of environmental threats, such as pollution, loss of habitat, and extinction of species. The 1960s were an important period for activism of all kinds and people from all walks of life rallied to support the environmental movement.[2]

The first Earth Day was held on April 22, 1970. Organized by a small group of activists, support for the first Earth Day was fed by media coverage. Word spread in the press and from person to person. On that first Earth Day, more than 20 million people across the United States took part in day-long activities to educate the public about environmental issues. So many people attended New York City's

Earth Day celebration that Fifth Avenue, one of the city's main streets, had to be closed to traffic. Across the nation, people cleaned up litter, handed out information, and demonstrated against factories that polluted land, water, and air.

At this time President Richard Nixon established the Environmental Protection Agency (EPA). Congress also passed such landmark legislation as the National Environmental Protection Act, the Clean Air Act, and the Clean Water Act.

In the late 1970s, the environmental movement slowed when a group of ranchers started the Sagebrush Rebellion. Angered over attempts to restrict cattle grazing on federal land, the Sagebrush

In 1962 Rachel Carson suggested that DDT damaged the eggshells of Robins (shown here) and other birds and warned of the dangers of pesticide use.

Rebellion tried to slow environmental reform. This slowing reached a near standstill during the Reagan administration (1981–1989) when President Reagan appointed two supporters of the Sagebrush Rebellion philosophy to key environmental positions. Anne Gorsuch Burford was appointed director of the EPA and James Watt became Secretary of the Interior. Attention to environmental problems was limited to regional or local issues, such as poor air quality in Los Angeles or Boston's polluted harbor.

Despite the government's position in relation to the environmental movement, public opinion polls in the 1980s showed that the environment was still a major concern for many Americans. Membership grew in grassroots and national organizations such as Greenpeace and the National Wildlife Federation. Local governments began to assert leadership on environmental issues, filling the gap left by the federal government.

Journalists continued to report on national and worldwide environmental problems, such as acid rain, deforestation, global warming (a dangerous increase in temperatures worldwide caused by a buildup of gases in the earth's atmosphere), pollution, species extinction, depletion of the ozone layer, and oil spills. People around the world grew more aware of environmental problems and realized that the future of the earth was tied to the decisions they made and actions they took every day. "We have a global economy," writes author Ruth Caplan in *Our Earth, Ourselves*. "How it operates will set the course either for future environmental devastation or for our being able to live within the bounds of our sustainable resources."[3]

Since the 1980s, the environmental movement has grown globally and locally. Many people now believe that the best approach to our use of the environment is conservation. The goal of conservation is to sustain our environment for future generations. Laws that were passed in the 1970s have been expanded and toughened. Still, upholding the law and conserving the environment takes money—money the federal government does not want to spend.

The Environmental Movement Today

Today, more than ever, protecting our environment is a major concern. Many people have rallied around a variety of environmental issues. According to the Internal Revenue Service, there are more than twelve thousand environmental nonprofit organizations in the United States. Companies have discovered that "going green"—modifying their own practices to become more environmentally responsible and supporting only responsible companies—pays in public approval and profits. But while some businesses help protect the environment, many others do not.

Environmental protection is a complex topic and there are many ways to look at the issues and much disagreement over the solutions. Environmental laws and regulations have impact on the local and national economy, employment, taxes, land development, housing, agriculture. Governments walk a fine line between meeting the needs of individuals and businesses and sustaining the environment. For example, if an environmentally damaging mining or lumber operation is closed down, it puts miners or loggers out of work and therefore affects the local economy. The proposed environmental benefits of an action must be weighed against its possible economic and social effects.

Also, environmental solutions must be global. Air pollution does not stop at national borders. One country's wastewater flows into another country's drinking water. Loss of rain forest in South America affects the climate in Europe. The people of the world must change if the world is to survive.

Conservation also creates conflicts between developed and developing nations. Industrialized countries like the United States that have advanced, prosperous economies can afford to promote environmental concerns. Poorer countries are more involved in trying to create industry and improve agriculture than in protecting the environment.

In 1992, world leaders met in Río de Janeiro, Brazil, and pledged to save our planet by introducing wide-ranging conservation policies in their countries. Unfortunately, none of these countries made good on its promises to the environmental movement. Since 1992, emissions of carbon dioxide and other gases that contribute to global warming have *increased* and could raise global temperatures as much as six degrees Fahrenheit by 2100; plant and animal species continue to become extinct each year. As a result, as many as one fifth of the world's population has no safe drinking water.[4]

Workers cleaning up an oil spill.

Unfortunately, there are no easy answers to environmental problems. This book will discuss some of the major environmental problems we face, explore solutions, and explain what each of us can do to help save our own small part of this planet.

2

How Many People Are Too Many People?

Until recently, it was believed that human population had only a small impact on the environment and that impact was usually localized. Today, however, people may be the most demanding challenge our environment faces. There are many environmental issues created by human population and overpopulation.

The current world population is 6 billion, and it is growing by twenty-three people every five seconds—that is almost four hundred thousand people a day, or 145 million people a year. By 2050, it is expected to pass the 9 billion mark.[1]

Population projections are performed

using assumptions about fertility (the birthrate) and mortality (life expectancy) to project future population size. But assumptions are educated guesses about what might happen and they can be far different from what really happens. In the past, demographers (people who specialize in the study of the statistical characteristics of the human population) projected huge swells in the population that have not occurred. Today, some experts believe that the population explosion is leveling off and may even decline in the future. In fact, total fertility rates in many industrialized countries are dropping, and the number of countries with a below-average fertility rate has tripled since 1970.

Population growth is measured by the total fertility rate of women—the average number of children each woman needs to bear to maintain the existing birthrate. In 1999, the worldwide total fertility rate was 2.1 children per woman. If the overall fertility rate goes below 2.1, population decreases. If it goes above 2.1, population increases.

A record number of young people around the world are now entering child-bearing years. Ninety percent of them live in developing countries that have the highest population growth in the world. Many of these countries have poor standards of living and lack basic necessities such as safe drinking water and medical care. Infant mortality is especially high. Women in impoverished nations also tend to have more children than women in wealthier nations. If the fertility rate continues unchecked in the next fifty years, India's population alone will soar from

930 million to 1.53 billion! This increase will "require a doubling of the world grain harvest and, for irrigation alone, a quantity of water equal to more than 20 Nile Rivers."[2]

How Population Affects the Environment

One of the keys to understanding the effects of population on the environment is to look at the number of people in an area relative to its resources. An area's resources set the limit on its ability to sustain human activities. An area is overpopulated when its population cannot be maintained without using up those resources that cannot be renewed, such as coal.

Historically, we have seen that the environmental impact of population growth can be gradual, but devastating. For example, El Salvador, a small Central American country, is facing ecological disaster primarily due to the stress caused by its 6 million people. El Salvador's dense rain forests have been reduced to rocks and sand. Loss of trees has contributed to increased average temperature and decreased rainfall. In some parts of the country, blue sky is obscured by gray smoke from burning fields and garbage. The devastation of the countryside has caused thousands of people to flee to the cities. In San Salvador, the capital, more than eleven thousand children die each year due to respiratory problems caused by polluted air, poor living conditions, and lack of medical care. This influx of people has also strained food and water supplies, creating water wars between local communities.[3]

There are no easy solutions when environmental and social problems reach these proportions. The forest cannot be replenished quickly. The land cannot be made fertile. Water cannot be made to fall from cloudless skies. What has happened in El Salvador could happen around the world if United Nations (UN) population projections about growth are correct.

But what happens if projections about *declining* population are correct? A different set of problems arises. For example, today China exports goods to the

These apartments in the Bronx, New York, sit near a garbage dump that has been filled past capacity.

United States and European countries, which helps the Chinese economy. With a declining population in the United States and Europe, China's exports will shrink and that will hurt it economically.[4]

How Population Increases Due to Migration

Sometimes, population in an area increases not due to birthrate but migration. It is the density of population in a given area that causes stress on the environment. As population increases due to migration, this stress increases, and we begin to see a negative impact on the environment. For example, more than 20 percent of the endangered Key deer population have been killed by automobiles, and recreational boats are the main cause of injury and death for Florida's endangered manatees. According to Anne Elizabeth Beale, deputy director of Population-Environment Balance, "Considering that the majority of the estimated 30,000 plant and animal species in the United States live near coasts where more than 50 percent of the human population also resides, massive habitat destruction is inevitable. The rate of species extinction in the United States will increase dramatically."[5]

A good example of how migration affects the environment can be found in the American Southwest, where the population has increased 98 percent in just twenty years, primarily due to migration. The vast Sonoran Desert, which extends into much of the southwestern United States and part of Mexico, is

Urban sprawl in Phoenix, Arizona. The population of Phoenix has grown primarily from migration.

home to species found nowhere else. Desert habitats are fragile, however, and the growth of the human population in the area has been devastating to this unique environment. Thirty-six bird species have vanished from the area and more than 2.5 million acres of plants have been killed off. This destruction of plant life has been blamed on water diversion due to the building of more than forty dams to serve farms and cities. Off-road vehicles have also damaged native vegetation and eroded soil. The introduction of nonnative grasses and other plants for cattle grazing has had a negative effect on the regeneration of native cacti, plus overgrazing of introduced cattle has diminished food sources for native animals such as bighorn sheep and pronghorns (antelope-like mammals).

What is happening in our deserts is not unique to the United States. Nations around the world face similar—and worse—environmental problems as they try to balance the needs of both people and the earth.

3

Lost Farmland Makes for a Hungry World

Farming is one of the world's oldest activities. The ability of the farmer to grow food for others is a major factor in the development of civilization. But farmers need rich soil, adequate water, good weather, and appropriate growing seasons. If any of these elements is missing or seriously affected, crop production is reduced.

In order to feed the world's billions, food production must increase. From 1950 to 1984, worldwide grain harvests were abundant. Many countries increased production by more than 50 percent, keeping ahead of population growth. In

1984, however, worldwide harvests began to decline and the amount of grain per person decreased. Weather contributed to some of the decline. Climate is a major influence on agriculture, and farmers suffer losses due to worldwide climate changes caused by pollution, flooding, drought, unseasonable rain, and temperature increases.[1] In 1999, flooding from Hurricane Floyd drowned livestock and destroyed crops in North Carolina. Farmers lost 100,000 hogs, 2.4 million chickens, and 500,000 turkeys. More than $243 million worth of crops were destroyed by the hurricane.[2]

The Loss of Farmland

Much arable land (land that can be used for growing crops) has been lost as cities grow and gobble up land for housing and industry. Groundwater (the water found underground) is diverted to cities and is no longer available for agriculture. Arable land is often planted with non-food crops, such as cotton and rubber trees. Cutting down trees and exhausting the nutrients in soil destroys the soil's fertility. According to the United Nations, about 59,570 square kilometers (23,000 square miles) of land worldwide—an area a little larger than the state of Maryland—becomes desert each year. Another 199,430 square kilometers (77,000 square miles) can no longer be farmed or support grazing.[3]

Many farmers in developing nations create agricultural land using a process called slash and burn. This involves burning trees, brush, and grass to clear a patch of land for planting. The ash left from the burning acts as a fertilizer and the soil produces crops for a few years. Often, the land is planted until it is exhausted and eroded and cannot support additional growth. More forests are burned and, eventually, the forest is gone and no arable land is available for farming. In the African Sudan, for example, poor farming techniques have severely degraded soil. A similar situation exists in Rwanda, another African country, and the Mexican state of Chiapas. Kazakhstan, in the former Soviet Union, has lost 50 percent of its arable land.[4]

Agricultural Chemicals Adversely Affect the Environment and People

Soil erosion can also deplete arable land. Soil erosion occurs when topsoil—rich organic material and nutrients needed for plant growth—is washed or blown away. Worldwatch Institute estimates that 20 billion tons of topsoil are carried away by rivers and streams each year. Since it can take up to a thousand years for one inch of topsoil to form, loss of topsoil is a major concern. To compensate for lost topsoil, farmers turn to fertilizers, which create environmental problems as they run off and pollute water and ecosystems.

Once upon a time, animal manure and compost were the primary sources of fertilizer. After World War I, the development and use of chemical fertilizers became common. Chemical fertilizers, however, are not environmentally friendly. For example, the nutrients found in chemical fertilizers can accumulate in water and promote excessive growth of algae in rivers, lakes, and bays. Algae crowd out other species and use up oxygen in the water. According to *State of the World 1998*, a Worldwatch Institute report: "Leached and eroded nutrients help make agriculture the largest diffuse source of water pollution in the Mississippi River. A 'dead zone' the size of New Jersey forms each summer in the Gulf of Mexico, where the Mississippi River empties."[5] This area of the Gulf has fewer fish and shrimp than other areas because the excessive algae use up available oxygen.

Fertilizers can also destroy land. Too much fertilizer can be toxic. For example, fertilizers applied to Minnesota grasslands helped the growth of some grasses but destroyed others, causing a 50 percent decline in species diversity.[6]

Human health is also affected. Nutrients such as nitrogen and phosphorus, which are found in chemical fertilizers, are dangerous to people. If ingested in water, they can contribute to a variety of illnesses, such as cancer and brain tumors; they can even cause death in infants. Nitrate pollution is one of the most serious water-quality problems in Europe and North America.

Pesticides are another environmental pollutant associated with agriculture. Annual farm losses due to pests can be as high as 40 percent of production. However, of the more than 544.3 million grams (1.2 billion pounds) of pesticides that are used each year, only 10 percent are effective.[7]

Pesticide pollution is a major environmental

Hazardous chemicals and radioactive waste must be labeled prior to disposal.

problem. Pesticides can contaminate water sources and kill wildlife. Chemical pollution poses great danger to birds. For example, more than 20,000 Swainson's hawks were inadvertently killed in Argentina in both 1995 and 1996, when farmers used a lethal pesticide on grasshoppers. The hawks were poisoned when they ate the grasshoppers. One of the worst chemical threats of the last sixty years was the pesticide DDT. Before its effects on birds, animals, and even people were understood, DDT was widely used. Its application in the United States has been phased out and banned, but it is still used in other parts of the world. DDT was meant to poison destructive insects, but when birds ate the poisoned insects, the DDT remained in their bodies. When the birds laid eggs, the eggshells were extremely thin. The eggshells broke open before the baby birds could survive. As a result, bird populations declined significantly.

Two pesticide chemicals believed to be responsible for much of the pollution of ground and surface water are diasinon and chlorpyrifos, sold under the brand name Dursban™. They are members of a family of chemicals similar to nerve gas, yet they are available in sprays, liquids, and dust forms in most hardware stores and nurseries. These pesticides are used in agriculture and around the home, in gardens and to eliminate household pests such as fleas and roaches. They are carried into creeks, rivers, and groundwater by rain and irrigation runoff. Here they contribute to the loss of wildlife, and they make people sick.[8]

Pesticides pose risks for people. The World Health Organization estimates that more than one million people suffer from pesticide poisoning each year. Children and young people are especially vulnerable to pesticides. According to the National Resources Defense Council: "Children are exposed to pesticides at home, schools, parks, and playgrounds and in food and water. Pesticides have been associated with children suffering from leukemia, sarcomas, and brain tumors, and can harm the nervous system."[9] Despite the dangers, a nationwide survey found that 85 percent of households owned at least one pesticide, sometimes stored within reach of children under the age of five.[10]

In 1999, in and around New York City, there were people who appeared to be suffering from encephalitis. Researchers believed that the virus that causes this disease was spread by mosquitoes. To keep this dangerous disease from spreading, the insecticide Malathion was sprayed from airplanes. Although the New York City Department of Health stated that there was no danger to children, it advised people to stay indoors during spraying because the insecticide could cause eye or skin irritations and adversely affect those with breathing problems.[11]

Solutions to Stop Loss of Cropland May Be Expensive

Cropland is a vital resource. Many nations have begun preservation programs to save millions of acres of farmland. New technologies can help prevent erosion and ensure productivity without damaging the environment.

In the United States, the federal government has created laws to control the use of dangerous agricultural chemicals. The Federal Agricultural Improvement and Reform Act of 1996 supports crop rotation, a nonpolluting technique to maintain productive farmland. The law provides $100 million a year for research and development and another $35 million in matching funds for state and local farm protection programs. The law also includes a program to reduce livestock pollution.

Many other federal laws help protect the environment by controlling the flood of new chemicals into the marketplace. One solution to the problem of agriculture-related pollution is to replace dangerous chemicals with organic and natural fertilizers and pesticides. Organic farming employs natural pest control. Natural pest control is a method that uses a pest's natural enemies, such as viruses and insect predators, to control the pest. Organic agriculture protects the health of the soil, conserves energy, reduces soil erosion, and does not contaminate water, air, or food.

Organic solutions can be expensive and are less convenient than chemicals. Still, organic foods are being grown by many major food manufacturers. If consumers are willing to pay higher prices for produce grown without pesticides, herbicides, and other manufactured chemicals, big business will take notice and take action.

Precision farming is another way to maximize production and reduce pollution. It uses a variety of high-yield farming methods. Farmers apply exact amounts of fertilizer, including manure, and herbicides only where they will do the most good to increase crops. The amount of pollutants put in the environment can be greatly reduced by this approach to farming.[12]

Large-scale modern agricultural techniques are not suited to rain forest land. In developing countries, a farming method called agroforestry combines modern technology and ancient knowledge about the rain forest to create food and protect the environment at the same time. Instead of clearing away the forest, the farmer works with it. With agroforesty, farmers raise a variety of traditional crops, such as maize, sweet potatoes, banana, cacao, or coffee trees, in alternating rows within the forest, among the trees. This prevents erosion, and fallen leaves from the trees serve as a natural fertilizer.[13]

Environmental advocates in developing countries are using creative techniques to educate people in new ways of farming. In Africa, puppet shows and radio programs spread information about sustainable agricultural methods. In India, Village Extension workers travel the countryside teaching new farming techniques. The United Nations Children's Fund sponsors a program that teaches village women to produce and process food.

A field of study in agricultural research called hydroponics could help us deal with shrinking amounts of land. Hydroponics, as its name suggests,

In many places throughout the world, people continue to rely on traditional farming techniques.

is a way of using water or moisture to grow plants without rooting them in the ground. Plants can be grown in tubes with aerated water and nutrients or held in bags in a moist room where they are continually sprayed with nutrients.

4

Trying to Get the Most Out of Energy Resources

Experts project that worldwide energy needs will increase as much as 400 percent in the next fifty years. A good part of that growth will come from the United States. Even though the United States has only 5 percent of the world's population, we use 25 percent of total worldwide energy. Most of the energy used in the United States comes from fossil fuels: 42 percent from oil, 24 percent from coal, 23 percent from natural gas, 7 percent from nuclear sources, and the remaining 4 percent comes from renewable sources such as wind and solar power. Only 20 percent of the energy used worldwide comes from renewable sources.[1]

Utility companies make electricity by burning fossil fuels such as coal, oil, and natural gas to power the generators that produce electricity. Fossil fuels are formed when heat and pressure react with the remains of plants and animals that died millions of years ago. Most fossil fuels come from deep within the earth's crust, and they can be reached only by drilling or mining. Fossil fuels are nonrenewable energy sources. It takes millions of years to create fossil fuels. And even though fossil fuels are still being created beneath the earth's surface, we are using more fossil fuels than are being created or that can be obtained. As a result, we may run out of fossil fuels in the future. If that happens, what do we do?

Nonrenewable fossil fuels also cause environmental problems such as air pollution and acid rain that damage trees, crops, and aquatic life around the world. When fossil fuels burn, they release chemicals such as carbon monoxide, carbon dioxide, and sulphur dioxide. These chemicals become trapped in the atmosphere where they contribute to air pollution and create smog, a haze that blocks sunlight.

Carbon dioxide (CO_2) and sulphur dioxide (SO_2) are called greenhouse gases because as they accumulate in the atmosphere they trap heat the way a greenhouse does. While a low level of greenhouse gases is necessary, when too much gas is present, too much heat is trapped in the atmosphere. This is called global warming and it is a major environmental problem.

One solution to the problems that result from using fossil fuels is to develop renewable sources of nonpolluting energy. Some types of renewable energy are solar, wind, geothermal, and biomass. Nuclear energy, another alternative, is a controversial one.

Renewable energy has drawbacks. It can be unpredictable—wind and sunlight cannot be guaranteed, for example. Costs for development and implementation can be high. Cost per watt of energy tends to be higher than with fossil fuels, and renewable energy gets less financial support from the government. In addition, a network of installations would have to be created in order to use renewable energy sources on a large scale.[2]

Solar Energy

The power of the sun can be used in a variety of ways. We now have the technology to use solar energy to light and heat buildings; we can also drive cars powered by solar-charged batteries. Solar energy is a clean, virtually unlimited energy source.[3]

More than two hundred thousand homes in the United States heat with solar energy. A passive solar building collects the sun's heat using large south-facing windows. Absorbers called sunspaces are used to capture and hold the heat during the day. When the temperature drops, the sunspaces release the trapped heat. Overhangs are used to control the amount of

A modular solar-heated house near Corrales, New Mexico.

sun trapped so that buildings are not overheated in summer.

The sun can also be used to heat water. Solar water-heating systems heat water and then store it until it is needed. Most homes that employ this heating method also need a conventional backup water-heating system since solar water heaters do not work well on cloudy days.

The sun's energy can even be used to make electricity. The process uses photovoltaic (PV) cells or solar cells. PV cells are nonpolluting. They are used to power satellites, electric lights, appliances, and even cars. PV cells are one of the world's fastest growing energy sources.

Solar thermal electric power systems change sunlight into electricity by using concentrated sunlight to heat water. The hot water creates steam that rotates a turbine, which in turn makes electricity using a generator.

Wind Power

Wind has been used for centuries to generate energy and electricity. Historically, windmills had many blades; modern windmills have only two or three blades, but they can be more than 24 meters (80 feet) long. The wind powers the blades, which drive a generator that produces electricity. Longer blades create more energy than shorter blades. In some places, large groups of windmills are connected to power lines and can produce power twenty-four hours a day—as long as the wind is blowing.

Wind is a highly viable alternative energy source. It is nonpolluting and, in many countries, the use of wind power is competitive with that of fossil fuels. It is also less costly than fossil fuel energy sources. Worldwatch Institute estimates that "wind turbines installed on .6 percent of the land of the 48 contiguous states, mainly in the Great Plains, could meet one-fifth of the current United States power needs."[4]

Geothermal Energy

Geothermal energy comes directly from the earth. Heat, formed by molten rock beneath the earth's surface, warms underground water in pools or geothermal reservoirs. When this water seeps to the surface of the earth, it forms hot springs or gushes like a geyser. One of the most famous examples of escaping geothermal energy is the Old Faithful geyser in Yellowstone National Park.

There was a time when we could harness geothermal energy only when it came to the surface of the earth. Now we can tap directly into underground geothermal energy by drilling wells. This provides steam that can be used to power generators and produce electricity. Geothermal energy has some drawbacks that are similar to other nonrenewable energy sources. Water in underground reservoirs may run out or be unable to replenish itself as fast as it is used. Plus, some geothermal reserves contain corrosive and polluting minerals.[5]

Old Faithful Geyser, Yellowstone National Park.

Water Power

Water in streams and rivers can be turned into hydroelectric power. The most common form of hydropower uses dams to send water through turbines, causing them to spin. The spinning turbines are connected to generators, which create electricity. A substation receives then transmits this electricity to homes and businesses.[6]

Hydroelectric power is used to provide electricity to entire regions of the country. It generates about 9 percent of all electricity in the United States and makes up 49 percent of all renewable energy in the country.[7] While hydroelectric power is nonpolluting, dams change the ecology of the area where they are built. Dams can disturb fish migratory patterns and wildlife habitats.

In some cases, dams can cause the destruction of wildlife habitats. For example, construction of the Bakun Dam in Borneo will require the destruction 170,000 acres of rain forest and flood an area of 570 square kilometers (220 square miles), the size of Delaware.[8] When their habitat is destroyed, wildlife may lose the areas they use to build homes and find food, and they could be easier targets for predators.[9] While the protection of wildlife is still being studied, the protection of fish has brought about new developments for dams. Two solutions devised to aid the fish migratory patterns are to create or redesign dams to have a steady stream flow or install fish ladders to help fish swim upstream to spawn.

Biomass

Biomass is a renewable energy source that is coming back into use, but in a different form. Biomass in the past came from burning wood. Today biomass energy is produced from manure, human sewage, plant matter, and landfill. Some biomass is salvaged from compost facilities and landfills and is burned to create clean energy. This kind of biomass currently provides 35 percent of the energy for developing countries.[10] Burning wastes helps to keep landfills from overflowing and actually absorbs carbon dioxide. While it reduces acid rain caused by sulfur emissions, it creates wastes in the form of ash and slag because of its contaminants.[11] Scientists are working on ways to reduce these contaminants so that the biomass produces less waste when burned. Another part of their research is to develop cleaner and more efficient fuels such as ethanol (a type of alcohol).[12]

Nuclear Solution or Nuclear Nightmare?

Another source of power is nuclear energy. Nuclear energy is created when atoms of heavy elements, such as uranium, are split. The process is called fission. It produces lighter elements and releases energy, which is used to generate electricity.

Some people think nuclear energy is clean and renewable. Nuclear energy does not pollute the air or contribute to smog or the greenhouse effect. It also cuts down the need to burn fossil fuels. But the by-products of nuclear fission are highly radioactive and dangerous to people and the environment. Nuclear power is a potentially dangerous and highly volatile way to obtain energy.

Nuclear power produces low-level and high-level radioactive waste. Generally, low-level radioactive waste is buried at special facilities. High-level waste may contain used nuclear fuel—highly dangerous radioactive material. Currently, used fuel in the United States is stored at nuclear power plants in pools of water or in concrete and steel containers.[13]

High-level radioactive material can be extremely dangerous and even lethal. Exposure to it can also cause cancer, delirium, cataracts, sterility, and birth defects in both humans and animals. The effects of radiation poisoning are long-term and diseases associated with it can occur thirty years after exposure.

Radioactive waste has a very long life before it decomposes. Some experts think that the containers used to store radioactive waste will decompose before the dangerous waste inside them decomposes. This could release radioactive waste into the environment.

Nuclear waste in other countries may not be as carefully stored, and there are real dangers of a nuclear accident occurring. Most nuclear reactors are supposed to be safe, but accidents do occur. The worst nuclear disaster in history occurred in Chernobyl, Ukraine, in 1986. Human error compounded by faulty technological design led to an explosion that ripped through reactor four of the Chernobyl nuclear plant. The accident released a poisonous radioactive cloud that drifted over the world and devastated the area around the explosion site. Thousands died from exposure to radiation, and more than ten years later radiation still contaminates wildlife and causes genetic defects in both people and animals in the area.[14]

Technology Provides Solutions

The electronics industry is moving steadily forward with a variety of innovations to save energy in personal computers, automobiles, and home and business energy systems. Some of these innovations are Intel's personal computer technology that wakes up computers from sleep mode faster so they operate

Nuclear power plants can provide tremendous amounts of energy, but remain controversial.

more efficiently. Canon has a system for laser printers that eliminates warm-ups and saves energy. Panasonic is focusing on improving automobile traffic control since about 11 percent of fuel vehicles use is wasted in traffic.[15] That wasted fuel adds to the smog level and pollutes the air everybody breathes.

5

Pollution and Climate Changes Cloud Our Blue Skies

As human population grows, so does pollution. Activities such as driving, farming, and manufacturing release chemicals into the atmosphere. These chemicals change our environment, poison the air, and degrade climate around the world.

Things Are Heating Up

Our planet is heating up! The winter of 2000 was one of the warmest winters on record.[1] While a variety of factors influence climate change, only one factor can be controlled—pollution.

Carbon dioxide gas and other gases,

such as methane and nitrous oxide, are released by automobiles and many industries. Thirty tons more of carbon dioxide are added to the air each year by burning fossil fuels and wood. These gases are called greenhouse gases. When they gather in the earth's atmosphere, they hold in heat like a greenhouse. The trapped heat warms the planet, and this warming may have serious long-term consequences. Deforestation—the destruction of forests around the world—increases the greenhouse gases by 20 percent.[2] Trees take in carbon dioxide from the air and give off oxygen in a process called photosynthesis. In this way trees and other plants clean the air and maintain a balance between oxygen and carbon dioxide in our atmosphere. When huge tracts of forests are destroyed, this natural control over the accumulation of dangerous gases is destroyed as well.

One consequence of the increase in temperature, called global warming, is the melting of the polar ice caps and glaciers. This melting will raise ocean levels and can lead to floods, storms, inundation of lowland areas, and extinction of plant and animal species. For example, a 1 meter (3.3 feet) rise in sea level would cover 80 percent of the Marshall Islands with water, displace 70 million people in low-lying Bangladesh, and threaten to flood the Japanese cities of Tokyo, Osaka, and Nagoya. Global warming could also create droughts and adversely affect agriculture in the Middle East, Africa, Australia, and parts of Latin America.[3]

The Growing Hole in the Ozone

Ozone is a gas naturally found high in the earth's atmosphere. Without the ozone layer, life could not exist on earth. It protects people from the sun's harmful ultraviolet radiation, which can cause skin cancer, cataracts, and weaken the body's immune system. As ozone is depleted in the upper atmosphere, experts predict a rise in these and other health problems.

Ozone depletion also interferes with photosynthesis, the way in which plants make food using sunlight, water, and carbon dioxide. The disruption of photosynthesis reduces agricultural production and increases carbon dioxide in the atmosphere, which, in turn, contributes to global warming and air pollution.

Ozone depletion can also damage marine life by causing the death of simple, microscopic, plantlike marine organisms called phytoplankton. Phytoplankton are at the bottom of the food chain; they serve as an important food supply for zooplankton (microscopic marine animals), fish, crustaceans, and some whales. If this simple basis of the food chain were damaged, entire species could become endangered or extinct. For example, baleen whales—right whales, gray whales, and humpback whales, among others—primarily eat phytoplankton and zooplankton. The largest baleen whale—the largest animal that has ever lived—is the blue whale, which can grow up to 30 meters (100 feet) long and weigh more than 143 tons. A reduction in the amount of plankton ultimately means decreased populations of these giants of the oceans.

Better Hold Your Breath

Factories, cars, and planes pour chemicals into the air. Even forest fires add dangerous chemicals to the mix. The polluted air that results is called smog. In some areas, the smog is so bad that the sky usually looks brown.

Air pollution can cause breathing problems, aggravate asthma, and contribute to the development of cancer and other diseases. In areas where rain forests are burning, the air is so polluted it can be deadly. Air pollution is especially bad for children, who inhale more pollutants per pound of body weight than adults.[4]

In the 1970s, Americans were breathing heavily polluted air. Today, we still are. Why? In 1970, people drove 1.8 trillion kilometers (1.1 trillion miles) a year, and in 2000 we will be driving more than 4 trillion miles a year. Although new cars are cleaner and pollute less than older cars, Americans are driving bigger cars for longer distances. For example, 1,400 sport utility vehicles roll off a single manufacturer's assembly line every day. Those 1,400 vehicles will release more than 6,600 tons of pollutants into the air each year. According to the Population Reference Bureau: "The growth in mileage simply outpaces the progress made in cleaning up tailpipe emissions, which produce more than half of all hazardous air pollution."[5]

What Goes Up Must Come Down—as Acid Rain

Acid rain is another environmental problem. When coal and gasoline burn, the chemicals they release mix with water vapor in the air and turn the water acidic—like vinegar. When this acidic water falls as rain, it is called acid rain, and it is harmful to people and the environment. Acid rain hinders photosynthesis and prevents plants from removing carbon dioxide from the air. Acid rain gets into lakes and rivers, pollutes habitats, poisons plants, and poisons animals

In urban areas, like New York City, smog is a daily problem.

and people who drink the water. The airborne chemicals in acid rain contribute to lung diseases, and long-term ingestion of contaminated water may cause health problems, including kidney disease and brain damage.

There has been some progress in reducing acid rain. A recent study looked at the levels of nitrates and sulfates, two of the main acids found in acid rain, in lakes and streams in North America and Europe. The study found that sulfate levels had decreased, suggesting that the damage caused by acid rain may not be permanent.[6]

Searching for Solutions

Climate is a complex issue that affects the entire planet. It can take decades before the impact of climatic changes can be measured and the causes identified. It could take centuries to correct. The solutions to global warming and ozone depletion must be international. Every country must put measures into place that control and, where possible, eliminate the emission of gases that contribute to these problems. This is especially challenging for developing countries where huge energy use is required for industrialization.

In 1997 representatives from 160 nations met in Kyoto, Japan, to seek solutions to world climate problems. They agreed to limit the production of dangerous gases that are contributing to major climate and atmospheric problems. Eighty-four of the nations present signed an agreement that calls for a

A scientist collects water samples for acid rain analysis in a Chesapeake wetland tributary.

reduction of greenhouse gases by at least 5 percent by 2012. Unfortunately, the United States has been reluctant to support the agreement and take the necessary steps to reduce the emission of greenhouse gases. Neither Congress nor the Clinton administration has taken steps necessary to control fossil fuel burning, promote energy efficiency, and support renewable sources of energy. How serious is the United States' failure to take action? Emissions of greenhouse gases in the United States are 10 percent higher than they were in 1990, and according to the Kyoto agreement, they need to be 7 percent lower in 2012 than they were in 1990. The longer the United States waits to begin reducing emissions, the more drastic the cuts must be in order to reach the goal set in Kyoto.

The United States is not the only nation holding up the progress of the Kyoto agreement. Developing nations such as China, South Korea, Indonesia, and India also need to control emissions aggressively. According to some experts, China will overtake the United States as the producer of the most greenhouse gases early in the twenty-first century. In order for the Kyoto agreement to succeed, worldwide cooperation is needed.[7]

While world powers decide how and when they will comply with the Kyoto agreement, new technologies, efficient energy sources, and energy standards can help reduce emission of deadly gases. Electric vehicles (EVs) offer clean transportation and can be a major factor in keeping the air free of fossil fuel pollutants. EVs are powered by electricity. In order to "fuel up," you plug your car into an electricity source. It will probably take years before enough consumers switch to EVs to begin to see a positive impact on the environment. As fossil fuels for gasoline become more scarce and more expensive, highly efficient EVs should become more popular.[8]

Taxes on fossil fuels like coal and gasoline and increased government subsidies for renewable energy sources and environmentally friendly transportation systems can also contribute to the solution. Pollsters report that many Americans support strong environmental regulations, but they do not necessarily want to be inconvenienced by these regulations. They do not want a healthy, safe environment at the expense of a healthy economy.[9]

6

Fresh Water?

Water is the most plentiful substance on our planet, covering more than 70 percent of the earth's surface. Made up of just two elements—hydrogen and oxygen—it circulates through evaporation, condensation, and rainfall in what is called the water cycle. In this way a constant amount of water is maintained, and it can be either fresh or salty.

Water is necessary for life. However, the ability of water to sustain life depends on its quality. Water quality is affected by several factors, such as the amount of acid, chemicals, and other substances in the water. Even though 70 percent of the earth is covered by water, less than 3 percent is fresh water, and most of that 3 percent is unavailable because it is glacial ice. Fresh water available for use is found mostly underground; a small amount is aboveground in lakes and streams.

Unfortunately, much of the fresh water on our planet has suffered from a variety of pollutants and other types of interference. Almost 20 percent of freshwater fish species worldwide have become either extinct or endangered.[1]

Water has two major kinds of uses. "Instream" use means using water in its natural environment. It includes water sports, commercial navigation, power generation, fishing, and sustaining wildlife habitats. The other type of use is "withdrawal." This involves removing water from streams or groundwater for consumption and agriculture. As population increases, experts expect water withdrawals to increase more than ten times by the middle of the next century. This is more than the earth's water supplies can support.

Water pollution is caused by industrial pollution, agricultural pesticides, and animal waste building up in bodies of water. Hard rains and flooding carry these pollutants from their source to fresh water lakes, streams, and rivers. Toxic materials included in landfill can seep into and pollute underground aquifers. Inadequate water supplies and poor water quality due to pollution are worldwide problems, especially for poor countries.

Environmental pollution and safe drinking water are a world-wide problem. Here, two girls are forced to bail their drinking water from a puddle in Lima, Peru.

Vulnerable Rivers

Rivers carry fresh water to larger bodies of water, such as oceans or lakes, and contain most of the fresh water that is available for human use. Rivers produce energy through hydropower generation, provide water to cool power plants, are major transportation routes for commerce, and are valuable as places to enjoy beauty and recreation.

Rivers are also an important habitat for a variety of wildlife. Fish such as trout, bass, salmon, and perch and many species of snakes, turtles, frogs, and insects call the river home. Beavers build their lodges in rivers, lakes, and streams, which also provide drinking water for wild animals and birds.

Currently, 40 percent of rivers in the United States are not clean enough for swimming or fishing. Rivers become polluted from sewage and industrial discharges, including toxic substances.[2] When the source of the pollution is distant from the actual polluted area, it is called nonpoint source pollution. For example, nonpoint source pollution occurs when a plant upstream releases a toxin that kills off fish downstream, as happened in the Hudson River in New York State. Nonpoint source pollution can occur across nations, making cleanup and accountability difficult.[3]

Agriculture is most often blamed and is a major factor in nonpoint source pollution. Agriculture accounts for much of the water use worldwide, and it is a leading contributor to water quality problems. Toxic pesticides used by many farmers can be washed from the fields when it rains and cause significant environmental damage.

Mining also contributes to water pollution. Chemicals, metals, and other harmful substances are washed away from mines and contaminate water supplies. Sulfuric acid can form from mine waste. The acid can dissolve metals and carry dangerous concentrations of dissolved metals with it. Special programs are aimed at reducing and/or eliminating mining pollutants, including acid mine drainage. However, the cleanup can be very expensive— upwards of $5 billion for one mine.

Water also runs off city streets and into rivers. This runoff carries oil, gasoline, and antifreeze from motor vehicles with it. These chemicals float on the top of the water and coat the feathers of birds. When they try to clean the oil and other chemicals off their feathers, they ingest these toxic substances and become sick; too often they die. Rivers can also become polluted with trash and litter. Animals eat the trash and get sick or die, or they become trapped in it and drown.

Pollution also comes from land use and development, forestry, and road building. With so many possible factors, it can be a major challenge to determine the cause of nonpoint source pollution. This can compound the problem and the make the cleanup more difficult.[4]

Twenty United States rivers have become so polluted that they are on a list of America's most endangered rivers, compiled by an organization called American Rivers. At the top of the list is the

Garbage dumps like this one can be a major source of pollution to rivers.

Hanford Reach, a stretch of the Columbia River that separates the states of Oregon and Washington. The second most endangered river is America's longest—the Missouri. According to Rebecca R. Wodder, the president of American Rivers, the Missouri is "little more than a stabilized barge canal that doubles as a storm sewer."[5] Pollution threatens many other rivers throughout the country, as well; from the Pocomoke and Potomac rivers in the east to the Fox and Kansas rivers in the central United States to the Walla Walla River in the west.[6]

Dams pose another kind of environmental challenge. They are built to control the flow of water in a river to generate electricity, for agricultural use, or to provide water for household or industrial use, often in distant areas. Damming rivers destroys natural habitats and permanently alters the course of the river and the quality of its water. Some experts believe that dams are a major cause of the extinction or endangerment of one-fifth of the world's freshwater fish. In addition, more than 30 million people around the world have been displaced by dam construction. When a dam was built on the Mun River in Thailand, for example, more than two thousand families were evicted from their homes, thousands more lost their source of food and income, and one hundred fifty species of fish disappeared from the river.[7]

The United Nations Industrial Development Organization (UNIDO) believes that cleaner industrial production techniques can decrease water pollution. UNIDO works with industries in developing countries to improve both production methods and water quality.

For example, UNIDO helped leather tanneries in Madras, India, develop cleaner technologies that eliminate nonpoint source pollution from manufacturing plants. In Mexico, UNIDO helped reduce water usage in the sugar cane industry by 95 percent.[8]

According to the Worldwatch Institute, "The key to stopping this needless destruction and repairing damage already done requires abandoning the fragmented approach to managing rivers and their watersheds. Integrated ecosystem-based planning [is needed] at the watershed, national, and international levels."[9] Great improvements can be made in river preservation. Already, better sewage treatment and industrial processes have eliminated some sources of pollution in most industrial nations.

The Mighty Oceans

Oceans are the great bodies of salt water that formed billions of years ago. More than 90 percent of all photosynthesis and release of oxygen occurs in oceans, which are highly productive environments for an incredible diversity of creatures. Oceans also provide a cost-effective way to transport goods from continent to continent. Ocean transportation is an industry that supports thousands of people worldwide.[10]

Ocean fishing is also a major industry. Many people fish the oceans to provide food for their families or to sell to distant markets. As a result of the fishing industry, many species of fish, such as salmon and tuna, have been depleted by over-fishing. The United Nations Food and Agriculture Organization estimates that two thirds of the world's fish stocks are beyond their sustainable level.[11] This decline not only affects the food supply for humans, it affects the entire food chain. For example, when over-fishing decimated walleye pollack in the North Pacific, the population of the Steller's sea lion, which feeds on the pollack, went into serious decline and is now listed as a threatened species.[12]

Since fish do not honor international borders, fishing can cause disputes among nations. Because nations are expanding their rights to offshore fishing and limiting trespassing by other nations, fish farming

The American dependence on fossil fuels has led to expensive ocean oil exploration.

is becoming an attractive alternative to ocean fishing. Fish farming allows people to depend on a readily available source of fish for food.

The ocean can also be a source of drinkable water. Even though the ocean is salty, the salt can be removed to create fresh water for human consumption and for agriculture. Although desalination (removing salt) is expensive, it is the best way to provide drinking water in some parts of the world.

The ocean is also a source of oil and minerals. Offshore oil production has increased and now represents a major part of the world's oil production. The ocean contains many valuable minerals, most of them on the ocean floor. When these minerals are mined, they provide a source of income for many nations. However, as with fishing, international territorial disputes often arise over which nation owns the mineral rights to deposits on the ocean floor.

Oceans are essential to the quality of life on earth, and yet they have become a dumping ground for waste. Shipping is a major source of pollution; ships dump waste and occasionally spill their oil in accidents. There are many ways oil can be spilled into the ocean—from ships that are transporting oil, from pipelines or oil wells, and from vessels that use oil for fuel. While most spills are relatively small, some large ones have caused catastrophic environmental disasters. When the *Exxon Valdez* oil tanker ran aground, it spilled 41.6 million liters (11 million gallons) of oil into the waters of Alaska's Prince William Sound. The Sound was rich in wildlife. The oil killed thousands of fish and birds and seriously damaged the food chain in this once pristine area. Even fish caught miles from shore showed evidence of contamination from the oil spill.

The United Nations Convention on the Law of the Sea and Agenda Twenty One call for international cooperation to manage marine resources. The Independent World Commission on the Oceans (IWCO) was created to assess the state of the oceans and establish priorities. According to Eduardo Faleiro, vice-chair of IWCO, "The sad fact though is that as much as we depend on the oceans for our very existence, they are being destroyed."[13]

Some European countries have strict nationwide standards for oceans. For example, the United

Oil scum in Prince William Sound, Alaska, one year after the Exxon Valdez *oil spill.*

Kingdom evaluates almost five hundred coastal beaches each year to determine if they meet national standards. The United States does not have such strict national controls and enforcement, so pollution from one state's coastal area can affect another state's coastline.[14]

7

The Shrinking
Land Beneath
Our Feet

Conservation of land is an important international environmental concern. As population increases, more people need more land for housing, business and industry, farming, animal grazing, and recreation. This means that land once called wilderness has become the latest subdivision, industrial park, golf course, or mall. These uses destroy habitats and contribute to a multitude of environmental problems, such as species extinction and water and air pollution. No habitat is safe from the effects of human development and the stresses of population growth.

Land is a nonrenewable resource. It

takes centuries to create a forest or wetland that supports a rich variety of wildlife. Once destroyed, it cannot be restored for generations. Wise land use that accommodates the compelling interests of people and sustains the land itself is an environmental goal and a challenge for nations around the world. It requires collaboration and long-term commitment.

The Importance of Wetlands

Wetlands are areas where the land is covered by water for all or part of the year. They are unique environments; many animal, plant, and insect species are found nowhere else. Coastal wetlands are areas where sea water from the ocean mixes with fresh water. Inland wetlands are areas such as swamps, bogs, marshes, and floodplains along rivers.

Wetlands are highly productive environments that are often compared to rain forests because of their immense variety of life. Wetlands are very important because they help maintain water quality by filtering runoff and reducing sediment and help control coastal flooding. During times of heavy rain and flooding, wetlands absorb water to help control flooding and help distribute water evenly over floodplains. Plants in wetlands store carbon instead of releasing it into the air as carbon dioxide. Migrating birds often choose wetlands to rest and feed and many people flock to wetlands to hike and observe the birds and wildlife. Wetlands even provide a wealth of products and food for human consumption

Wetlands are vital elements in many ecosystems.

and use, such as fish, shellfish, blueberries, cranberries, and wild rice.

Despite the value of wetlands, we lose about 90,000 acres of wetlands in the United States each year. In California 91 percent of the state's wetlands have been lost. While draining wetlands for agriculture has declined, development accounts for a large percentage of the loss, and what has not been converted during development is polluted.[1]

Rain Forests

Most of the world's tropical rain forests are found in the Amazon basin of South America, in areas of Africa, and in the islands of Southeast Asia. Temperate rain forests are found in higher latitudes, such as the northwest coast of North America, Chile, Tasmania, and parts of New Zealand and Australia.

Rain forests cover less than 6 percent of the earth's surface, but more than 70 percent of its plant and animal species are found in them. Approximately 40 percent of all medicines come from natural sources, and many of these are rare and unusual plants found only in rain forests. The National Cancer Institute spends millions of dollars collecting rain forest plants and studying their properties to see if they can cure diseases. For example, a promising drug for ovarian and breast cancer was discovered to be a component in the Pacific yew tree of North America. The yew had usually been discarded as trash; its wood is of no particular commercial value. Currently, scientists have studied only about 5,000 of the 25,000 species of flowering plants in rain forests. As we destroy forests and plant habitats, we are probably throwing away a vast source of medicinal drugs.[2]

Tropical rain forests are also natural "supermarkets" that give us many foods, such as coffee, cocoa, sugarcane, bananas, pineapples, papayas, cashews, Brazil nuts, and peanuts.[3]

Despite their unique value, rain forests are being destroyed around the world by commercial logging and clear-cutting for housing, agricultural, ranching, and fuel purposes. People destroy 1.5 acres of rain forest every second. How many seconds will it take you to read this page? How many acres of rain forest will be destroyed in that amount of time? According to current estimates, one half of the world's rain forests have already been lost.[4]

The relationship of trees to worldwide environmental health is just beginning to be appreciated—unfortunately too late to save huge tracts of forest around the world. The loss of rain forests is irreparable and has not only local but worldwide consequences.

When the rain forest is destroyed, the land on which it stood cannot support life. Without a protective canopy of trees, the hot sun bakes the ground. Moisture dries up, and when it rains, the rain beats directly onto the ground and carries away topsoil. Some experts think that huge portions of lush rain forests could become deserts due to erosion, which is twenty to thirty times worse in logged regions.[5] Trees remove carbon dioxide from the air and give off oxygen as photosynthesis occurs. Rain forests are a

Akaka Falls in a Hawaiian rain forest.

natural source of oxygen. As the number of trees decreases worldwide, oxygen decreases, carbon dioxide increases, and global warming occurs, which has negative environmental effects around the world.

Trees also help regulate the climate through transpiration, a process in which water vapor is released through pores on a tree's leaves. This vapor joins with vapor from surface water to form clouds that eventually drop moisture in the form of rain. Deforestation affects the amount of vapor contributed to rainfall and, with less rainfall, water supplies and agriculture are negatively affected.

Deforestation is an especially difficult issue for developing countries. By clearing rain forests, countries can provide agricultural land for growing food. The sale of the timber can also help poor nations. However, rain forest land is not arable and does not support crops for very long. Plots of land have to be abandoned after a few years. More forest is then cleared for planting until it, too, becomes unsuitable for agriculture, and the process starts over.

Construction of highways into the rain forest has also opened this fragile environment to other kinds of development. Logging and cattle ranching contribute to loss of habitat. Loggers cut down entire sections of forest and sell the timber to industrialized nations. What kind of wood products do you have in your home? Oak, pine, and maple come from temperate forests. Teak, rosewood, mahogany, and cedar can come from tropical rain forests.[6]

Converting rain forest to pasture for cattle is another problem. In just twenty-five years in Central

A controlled clear-cut in Hoh rain forest, Oregon. This small clear-cut section will help maintain biodiversity in the rain forest.

America, the amount of forest converted for grazing has doubled. World meat production has soared since 1950. This has been accompanied by increased consumer demand for animal byproducts, such as eggs and milk. But rain forest land makes for poor grazing, and after a few years the land wears out and more forest must be cleared.[7]

Saving Our Land for the Future

Land preservation is occurring on many fronts. In the United States, laws require that an environmental impact report be prepared for any development. The Clean Water Act protects wetlands and requires wetland restoration. Many states have additional protective regulations that govern wetlands use and activities. Education is also an important element, especially since 75 percent of wetlands are privately owned and the actions of individual landowners is critical to maintaining this fragile environment.[8]

Wetland mitigation is a tool for balancing development and wetlands preservation. Wetland mitigation is used when a necessary land development will have a negative impact on wetlands. In this process, the party that wishes to develop the wetlands must purchase and restore or create another equivalent amount of wetlands elsewhere and protect it, effectively replacing one wetland with another.

Mitigation "banks" can help restore and protect large areas of land. A mitigation bank buys, restores, and manages damaged wetlands. In return, the bank gets "credits" from the state based on the improvements it has made. When a developer's project negatively affects wetlands, the developer can use these credits to offset the negative impact. For example, if a highway construction project will affect wetlands, the state's department of transportation can set up a mitigation bank. The bank creates or restores wetlands in areas not affected by the construction project and builds up credits, which can be drawn on to offset wetlands damaged during the highway construction.[9] In this way, even though some wetlands are destroyed, other wetlands are created or saved.

One solution to deforestation is to develop plantations of trees that can be harvested for fuel and building materials. Cultivating trees specifically for timber means that wild trees and forests will not be cleared. Another solution is recycling. For example, the paper industry uses wood and paper recycling to reduce the demand for timber. Currently, only 40 percent of paper is recycled worldwide.[10]

The United States has a long history of preserving land in national parks and other types of preserves. The movement to create national parks began in 1870 with the naming of Yellowstone as the first national park in the United States. Other nations have followed our example; today more than two thousand national parks and preserves have been established in more than one hundred countries around the world.

The National Wildlife Refuge System is a collection of refuges totaling 93 million acres set aside for wildlife management and preservation. Managed by the United States Fish and Wildlife Service, it is the

Deforestation can lead to erosion. This area is now part of San Isabel National Forest, Colorado.

world's most comprehensive system of wildlife protection and land management. Refuges can be found from Alaska to the Florida Keys to the Hawaiian Islands. Refuges offer protection for more than 200 endangered species like whooping cranes and red wolves as well as hundreds of other species.[11]

Refuges are actively managed to meet the needs of diverse species. For example, controlled burning, thinning of forested areas, and cutting of grasslands helps new plants grow and creates food and nesting cover. Refuges provide habitat where wildlife can find food, shelter, water, and space.

Refuges are not just for wildlife. More than 30 million people visit refuges each year. They come to observe, learn, and enjoy nature. Most refuges have visitor centers and sponsor educational activities. Many use volunteers to conduct wildlife population surveys, lead tours, and assist with special projects, such as bird banding.

Bird banding is one of the most important ways scientists can study birds without having to kill them or keep them in captivity. Wild birds are caught and a numbered aluminum band is attached to one leg. Each band's number is entered into a nationwide database. If the bird is captured again later, or if it dies and its body is recovered, that information about the bird is entered into the database. Banding lets scientists collect and keep track of information like a bird's age and life span, migration patterns, population size, and more. This record can tell us a lot about how birds are affected by changes in the environment.[12]

Eco-tourism is another important way of conserving nature and it is one of the most popular forms of vacationing around the world. Countries are preserving their natural resources and promoting some of them as vacation destinations. Many of these destinations are located in fragile habitats, so nations must maintain a balance between commerce and conservation.

Travel and tourism is a major contributor to the economic growth of many nations. The motto of eco-tourism is "recycle, reuse, reduce." According to Geoffrey Lipman, president of the World Travel and Tourism Council, "Travel and tourism is in a unique position to spread the environmental message because it has the means to influence products and services provided by its suppliers. It is also in a position to educate its customers."[13]

As more and more land is set aside in parks and other protected reserves, miners, farmers, and developers feel the squeeze of having their livelihoods threatened. This pressure can create an adversarial relationship between them and conservationists. Many nations are trying to integrate the needs of both by addressing conflicting issues in the planning process and by multiple land use that allows for controlled exploitation of natural resources along with preservation of the environment.

Biosphere reserves are a new solution to meeting conflicting demands. In an area that needs environmental protection, a biosphere is set up with three zones. The first zone is the core area, which is devoted to long-term protection of habitat. The second zone is a buffer zone that supports activities such as

The delicate Prince William Sound is just one of many
threatened ecosystems that is now a tourist destination.

research and eco-tourism. The third and outermost zone is a transition area where the needs of local communities are addressed.

Biospheres conserve biodiversity and protect threatened habitats and ecosystems. They are models of land management and sustainable development that also support local people and meet their needs. For example, Kenya's Amboseli Biosphere Reserve was created around an existing popular tourist area. To provide water for both large wild mammals such as elephants and the domestic cattle owned by local Masai tribes, the biosphere dug wells in the transition zone. The Amboseli Biosphere Reserve also shares the profits generated by tourism with local communities.

The Maya Biosphere Reserve in Guatemala protects the tropical rain forest and provides local Indians with opportunities for income. They gather and sell chicle sap, xate leaves, and allspice. In this way, the forest has become an economically self-sustaining environment. As many Guatemalans now realize, it can be more profitable to sustain the forest than to destroy it.[14]

Waste Not, Want Not

Garbage. Sewage. It's all waste, and it has to go somewhere. The problem is *where?* More than 90 percent of waste is still deposited in landfills.

For years, landfills provided a way to safely dispose of solid waste. To prevent leaching into the ground, clay is used to line the landfill. Garbage is spread in layers and compacted. Then, a layer of soil is spread over the garbage and this is further compacted. Eventually, the area is filled to the top and is planted over. The nation's landfills are reaching capacity, and while large incinerators are now being used to dispose of waste, they create hazardous gases and toxic ash, which can only be disposed of in *another* landfill.

Landfills can pollute underground reservoirs of water. As rain seeps through the landfill it dissolves metals and chemicals from the material in the landfill and carries them into the soil and water sources. This is a major factor in nonpoint source water pollution.[15]

Space for new landfill is limited and this has fueled the movement toward waste management— reducing and controlling the amount of waste that actually needs to be disposed of through a variety of recycling programs. For example, about one third of waste is composed of paper, glass, metals, and plastic, which are recyclable. Another 30 percent comes from yard and food waste, all of which is biodegradable. Waste can even be used as energy. When organic matter decomposes, it can be used to generate electricity. In other words, more than half of our waste is not waste at all.[16]

Recycling protects the environment, creates jobs, and provides the opportunity for growth industries. It can even be a moneymaker. Discarding garbage, sewage, and manure from cities and animal facilities is a waste of natural resources since organic materials can be converted into usable products. Once this

Landfills such as this one of discarded car parts, can be a major source of pollution.

waste has been treated to make it safe, it can be sold to farmers as fertilizer. This use reduces the need for chemical fertilizers that allow the runoff of dangerous chemicals.

Today, California composts 40 percent of its organic waste; more than 30 percent of sewage sludge in both Europe and the United States is recycled.[17] However, much more needs to be done. We are still throwing away too much reusable waste.

8

Biodiversity Enriches Our Earth

The great variety of plant and animal life on earth is described as "biodiversity." Sustaining biodiversity is essential to the survival of our planet. Every animal, insect, bird, fish, and plant is beautiful and plays some role in our survival.

Scientists have identified about 1.75 million species worldwide so far. Many experts believe that more than 30 million different species may exist. This means that we have barely dented the surface of the world's diversity. Unfortunately, many of these species may become extinct before we have a chance to discover and study them. Experts estimate that one out of every four species will become extinct in the next fifty years. The rate of extinction for dinosaurs was one species every ten thousand years.[1]

How important is one type of animal or plant in the big picture? Each species is important. Eighty percent of the world's crops and one third of United States agricultural output depend on pollinators like bees, insects, bats, and birds, whose populations are in jeopardy. In the United States more than half of our honeybee colonies have been lost since World War II. Most people know that honey is the main product we get from bees, but their pollination services are worth more than their honey.[2]

All of the fruits and vegetables we consume today were cultivated from wild species. After many years of cultivation, domestic fruits and vegetables have become susceptible to diseases. We need to use their wild ancestors to obtain sturdier genetic materials to strengthen domestic plants.[3]

According to Ed Clebsch, a professor of botany, "For every single species that becomes extinct, fourteen others will eventually go with it."[4] Why? The loss of a single species creates a domino effect, affecting every other species that depends on it.

Causes of Extinction

Extinction of species is a naturally occurring event resulting from geologic and climatic changes. Today, extinction also occurs because we are destroying natural habitats or, in some cases, deliberately killing animals themselves. Every habitat on earth is in

The endangered Sea Turtle cruises a coral reef in the Florida Keys.

danger: rain forests, coral reefs, salt marshes, wetlands, deserts, tundra—the list goes on and on.

How are habitats and individual species threatened? As population grows, people need food, shelter, clothing, and energy. In industrialized countries, people also demand conveniences such as automobiles and air-conditioning. These needs often conflict with the desire to protect the environment. The long-term harm of environmental destruction, however, far outweighs the short-term benefits gained. As habitats such as forests, wetlands, and coral reefs are altered, entire ecosystems are destroyed.

Habitats support entire ecosystems. When they are damaged, the effects can be catastrophic. For example, entire desert habitats in the American Southwest have been replaced by crops, housing, golf courses, and resorts. Where kit foxes and elf owls once hunted, golf carts now roam. In these areas, domestic livestock compete with wild animals for grazing land and drinking water. Competition is especially fierce in arid areas. Wildlife often lose this battle and simply disappear. As wild lands shrink due to urban development, animals such as bison, wolves, and bears wander out of protected areas and "trespass" into human territories where they can be hunted and exterminated.

Pollution also contributes to extinction. Frogs and salamanders are natural predators of mosquitoes and other insects that spread diseases. Pollutants such as acid rain can kill these amphibians and other aquatic animals. If these predators disappear, insect pests will proliferate. More than twenty varieties of clams and thirty types of fish are currently threatened by pollution.[5] A buildup of salt in one Mexican lagoon contributed to the deaths of ninety-four endangered sea turtles.

Superstition even can lead to the extinction of some animals. The wolf is one good example. Many legends talk about people turning into vicious werewolves who attack and kill. Negative superstitions like this one have helped make wolves the target of a concerted extermination effort. They have been shot, poisoned, and trapped. The red wolf became extinct in the wild in the 1970s. Today, some species of wolves are being reintroduced into their old strongholds in the United States.

Other animals are victims of exploitation. Whales have been hunted almost to extinction to make a variety of "necessary" items, such as dog food. Some cultures believe that rhinoceros horn can be made into a love potion. Many poachers kill rhinoceroses just for their horns. The high price of ivory has led to the near extinction of the African elephant, which has been hunted for its ivory tusks. Even today, despite laws that are supposed to protect these animals, whales, rhinos, elephants, and scores of other endangered and threatened animals are killed by poachers.[6]

Dealing in exotic species can also be big business, and any time there is money to be made, unscrupulous people will break the law. Smuggling of wildlife is a $6-billion-a-year industry according to the United States Justice Department. Collectors will pay

The United States had a long tradition of whale hunting, until over-hunting nearly made many species extinct. Even today, some countries still hunt whales.

more than $30,000 for a rare or endangered creature. Millions of animals and plants are poached each year to meet the demand.[7]

Invasion by alien species can also lead toward species extinction. Aliens are all around us and they are not from outer space. Alien species are plants and animals that are not native to a region but have been introduced into it. They are called "exotic" species. As people migrate, they bring exotics with them either on purpose or inadvertently. Exotics often flourish in their new environment because they have no natural predators. As they thrive, they crowd out and destroy native species. For example, early ships coming to Hawaii were often infested with rats. The rats had no natural predators, and their population soared. To control the rats, mongooses were introduced. Unfortunately, mongooses developed an appetite for more than rats—native Hawaiian animals and birds quickly fell prey to these voracious predators. Now, the challenge is to control both the rat and the mongoose populations and still protect native wildlife.

Ways to Save Wildlife

There are several solutions to the challenge of sustaining biodiversity around the world. National and international laws are required to protect endangered species. The Convention of International Trade in Endangered Species (CITES) of Wild Fauna and Flora became official in July 1975. One hundred forty-three nations have banned commercial international trade in animals on a list of endangered species. They also regulate and monitor trade in other species that are threatened with extinction.

In the United States, the goal of the Endangered Species Act is to restore species to the point where they no longer need protection. Recovery plans have been created for almost one thousand species. Each plan identifies actions that will help the species recover, including reintroducing the species into a recovered or new habitat, captive breeding, land acquisition, and technical assistance for landowners.

Zoos and botanical gardens are now preserves for the breeding of endangered and threatened animal and plant species. Today, zoos are on the forefront of the movement to save species. They are creating banks for frozen sperm and eggs from endangered species. They also use a variety of techniques such as artificial insemination (introducing a male's sperm into a female's body without sexual contact) and in vitro fertilization (bringing together egg and sperm outside the animal's body; the fertilized egg is then implanted into the uterus) to propagate species. More than 90 percent of the animals in zoos have been bred in captivity. The American Zoo and Aquarium Association has a database of 255,000 captive animals around the world. This database is used to match prospective mates with the goal of propagating species.[8]

Once upon a time, zoos snatched animals from the wild and threw them into tiny metal cages. Zoos and aquariums are moving away from traditional cages and building habitats that replicate the animal's

The endangered spotted owl.

natural environment. In many cases, visitors are the ones in cages. Wildlife parks let the animals run free while people ride around in enclosed cars. The Bronx Zoo has a monorail and cable cars that allow people to view animals from above.

Not all zoo animals spend their lives in captivity. Many zoos and aquariums have programs to introduce captive-bred animals into the wild, provided their natural habitat is restored and can support them. The animals must be taught how to be wild and are monitored to ensure that they can take care of themselves and become integrated into their environment. The black-footed ferret is a good example of how the program works. Currently, this ferret is one of America's most endangered mammals. Thanks to a program at the Phoenix Zoo, ten of these once numerous animals are again fending for themselves successfully in the wilds of northern Arizona. The National Zoo's Conservation and Research Center in Front Royal, Virginia, is raising endangered Asian wild horses, the world's only species of wild horse. Today, thirteen of the remaining horses are learning survival skills in the hopes that one day captive-bred Asian wild horses may again roam the steppes of Mongolia.[9]

National parks and refuges are key to sustaining biodiversity, and they can also be a source of income, especially for cash-strapped developing nations. According to Jeff McNeely, chief scientist for the World Conservation Union, "A protected area is not only a natural resource, it is an economic resource."[10] For example, the Kenya Wildlife Service charges $27 a day per person for tourists to visit its wildlife park, and the Uganda Wildlife Authority charges more than $150 for the privilege of seeing a rare mountain gorilla in the wild. The Natal Parks Board that governs Kruger National Park in South Africa has been merging economics and conservation for years and is thriving. About 37 percent of its $35 million annual budget comes from business activities, and the percentage is expected to increase.[11]

9

Helping to Heal an Imperfect World

It is said that a butterfly flapping its wings in a South American rain forest can affect traffic patterns in London. All life on earth is connected. No person, animal, plant, insect, fish, or bird lives in isolation. Nature is not as pure or clean as it was centuries ago. Actions taken today affect the environment today and tomorrow and, sometimes, for generations. If people are wasteful, careless, or apathetic about their environment, they will simply continue the negative actions of the past. If they recycle and are mindful of their environment, their positive actions can help heal the injuries of the earth.

An eroded shoreline on the sea islands of Georgia.

Do not let all the problems of the environment overwhelm you into doing nothing. Simply try to do what you can. Make decisions that support the environment. Refuse to buy products that contribute to pollution or waste. Recycle and reuse whenever possible. Follow the news to find out what is happening to the environment both locally and globally. Write your congressional representatives and senators to express your concerns. Find out what their record is on environmental issues. How do they vote on bills that have environmental impact? Encourage your family and older friends to vote for candidates with strong environmental platforms.

You can also join organizations such as Greenpeace, the Sierra Club, the National Wildlife Federation, and others that are dedicated to preserving the environment and solving environmental problems. By joining organizations that help the environment, you help continue their rewarding work and you are more likely to have an impact.

We only have one world and we will benefit by preserving it. It is up to us—we caused the problems, and we must come up with the solutions. Be aware and take action.

Chapter Notes

Chapter One. "Going Green": The Environmental Movement

1. Traci Watson, "The End of an Arctic Paradise," *USA Today*, <http://www.exxonvaldez.org/usatoday4. html> (May 24, 1999).

2. "The Roots of Modern Environmentalism," *National Resources Defense Council*, March 5, 1997, <http://www.nrdc.org/nrdc/bkgrd/greenvhis.html> (December 7, 1999).

3. Ruth Caplan and the staff of Environmental Action, *Our Earth, Ourselves* (New York: Bantam Books, 1990), p. 6.

4. Elliot Diringer, "Five Years After Earth Summit, Leaders Take Stock," *San Francisco Chronicle*, June 20, 1997, pp. A1, A11.

Chapter Two. How Many People Are Too Many People?

1. Ruth Caplan and the staff of Environmental Action, *Our Earth, Ourselves* (New York: Bantam Books, 1990), p. 247.

2. *State of the World 1998: A Worldwatch Institute Report on Progress Toward a Sustainable Society* (New York, W. W. Norton & Co., 1998), p. 174.

3. Edward Hegstrom, "Smoke Covers the Blue in El Salvador," *San Francisco Chronicle*, June 1, 1998, pp. A-8, A-10.

4. Barbara Crossette, "How to Fix a Crowded World," *The New York Times on the Web*, November 2, 1997, <http://search.nytimes.com> (May 18, 1998).

5. Tony Davis, "How Urban Sprawl Is Affecting Natural Resources in the Southwest," *The Earth Times*,

March 23, 1998, <http://www.earthtimes.org/mar/ environmenthowurbansprawlmar23_98.htm> (June 3, 1998).

Chapter Three. Lost Farmland Makes for a Hungry World

1. Don Hinrichsen, "Dangerous Trends in Food Production Threaten Development," *The Earth Times*, December 14, 1997, <http://www.earthtimes.org/dec/ foodsecuritydangerousdec14_97.htm> (March 16, 1998).

2. Roland Jones, "Rains Add to Floyd's Woes," *ABCNEWS.com*, September 23, 1999, <http:// abcnews.go.com/sections/business/DailyNews/ floydcommodities990922.html> (October 22, 1999).

3. "New Threats to Human Security: Study Documents Causes of 'New World Disorder'," Worldwatch Institute press release, October 24, 1996, <http://www.worldwatch.org/alerts/pr961024.html> (December 7, 1999).

4. Ruth Caplan and the staff of Environmental Action, *Our Earth, Ourselves* (New York: Bantam Books, 1990), pp. 242–45.

5. *State of the World 1998: A Worldwatch Institute Report on Progress Toward a Sustainable Society* (New York: W. W. Norton, 1998), p. 100.

6. Ibid.

7. Caplan, p. 120.

8. Jane Kay, "Poisons for Home," *San Francisco Examiner*, March 29, 1998, p. E4.

9. Jane Kay, "Kids Twist in Toxic Turmoil," *San Francisco Examiner*, November 25, 1997, p. A6.

10. "What is Children's Environmental Health?" *Children's Environmental Health Network*, May 1997, <http://www.cehn.org/cehn/About.html> (December 7, 1999).

11. "St. Louis Encephalitis: FAQ," *NBC4: Encephalitis in New York City*, September 10, 1999

<http://www.msnbc.com/local/wnbc/514820.asp>
(October 22, 1999).

12. "Report Card on Precision Farming," *The Futurist*, April 1998, pp. 8–9.

13. Christina G. Miller and Louise A. Berry, *Jungle Rescue: Saving the New World Tropical Rain Forests* (New York: Simon and Schuster, 1991), pp. 90–95.

Chapter Four. Trying to Get the Most Out of Energy Resources

1. Tracey C. Rembert, "Electric Current," *E: The Environmental Magazine*, November–December 1997, p. 30.

2. Ibid.

3. "Learn About Renewable Energy," Consumer Energy Information: EREC Fact Sheet, October 1995, <http://www.eren.doe.gov/erec/factsheets/rnwenrgy.html> (December 7, 1999).

4. "Wind Power Fastest Growing Energy Source Ready to Displace Coal, Slow Climate Change," August 14, 1996, Worldwatch Institute press release, n.d., <http://www.worldwatch.org/alerts/pr960814.html> (February 24, 2000).

5. "Learn About Renewable Energy."

6. "Hydroelectric Power: Turning Water's Mechanical Energy into Electricity," The National Renewable Energy Laboratory, December 1998, <http://www.nrel.gov/lab/pao/hydroelectric.html> (October 10, 1999).

7. Ibid.

8. "Learn About Renewable Energy."

9. "How a Hydroelectric Project Can Affect a River," The Foundation for Water and Energy Education, n.d., <http://www.fwee.org/hpar.html> (February 24, 2000).

10. Rembert, p. 34.

11. "Biomass Power Research: Making Electricity from Trash and Other Biomass Resources," <http://www.

nrel.gov/lab/pao/biomass_power.html> (December 7, 1999).

12. Ibid.

13. "Nuclear Energy Basics—Energy and You," Nuclear Energy Institute, n.d., <http://www.nei.org/basics/eay_main.html> (February 24, 2000).

14. Larry LaMatte, "Chernobyl 10 Years Later: A Threat to the Future," *CNN Interactive World News*, April 4, 1996, <http://www.cnn.com/WORLD/9604/04/cnnp_chernobyl/index.html> (August 7, 1998).

15. Randy Showstack, "'Smart' Technologies Cut Greenhouse Gas Emissions and Make Profit," *The Earth Times*, August 19, 1998, <http://www.earthtimes.org/aug/business_investingsmartaug19_989.htm> (September 9, 1998).

Chapter Five: Pollution and Climate Changes Cloud Our Blue Skies

1. "Damage to Nature Now Causing Widespread 'Natural' Disasters, Economic Hardship," Worldwatch Institute press release, February 11, 1997, <http://www.worldwatch.org/alerts/pr970211.html> (December 7, 1999).

2. "Global Warming: Focus on the Future," *Planetvision*, n.d., <http://host.envirolink.org/edf/index.html> (August 6, 1998).

3. William K. Stevens, "If Climate Changes, Who Is Vulnerable? Panels Offer Projections," *The New York Times on the Web*, September 30, 1997, <http://search.nytimes.com> (March 12, 1998).

4. "What Is Children's Environmental Health?" *Children's Environmental Health Network*, May 1997, <http://www.cehn.org/cehn/About.html> (December 7, 1999).

5. Robert Livernash and Eric Rodenburg, *Population Change, Resources & the Environment* (Washington: Population Reference Bureau, 1998).

6. "Signs of Recovery from Acid Rain," *CNN*, October 18, 1999, <http://cnn.com/NATURE/9910/18/acid.rain.enn/index.html> (October 22, 1999).

7. Anne Silverstein, "Nations Make Roll Call on Signing of Kyoto Climate Change Protocol," *The Earth Times*, April 24, 1999, <http://earthtimes.org/apr/nationsmakerollcallapr24_99.htm> (May 24, 1999).

8. "My Other Car Pollutes," *Via*, September/October 1998, p. 12.

9. "Future Will See Growing Gap in Clean Air Benefits of EVs and Gasoline," *Science and the Environment*, September 1996, <http://www.cais.com/publish/stories/0996air2.htm> (September 1, 1998).

Chapter Six. Fresh Water?

1. "Ocean Facts on Runoff Pollution," International Year of the Ocean, n.d., <http://www.yoto98.noaa.gov/facts/pollut.html> (December 7, 1999).

2. Barry Lewis, "Nonpoint Sources Part 2: Lifestyle Decisions Can Have Serious Effects," The Academy of Natural Sciences—Philadelphia, May 1996, <http://www.acnatsci.org/erd/ea/10nps2.html> (March 12, 1998).

3. Robert Livernash and Eric Rodenburg, *Population Change, Resources & the Environment* (Washington: Population Reference Bureau, 1998).

4. "Nonpoint Source Pollution: The Nation's Largest Water Quality Problem," Pointer No. 1, EPA, n.d., <http://www.epa.gov/OWOW/NPS/facts/point1.htm> (August 16, 1998).

5. C. Gerald Fraser, "Farm Animal Waste Threatens U.S. Rivers and Wildlife," *The Earth Times*, April 20, 1998, <http://www.earthtimes.org/apr/environmentfarmanimalwasteapr20_98.htm> (August 16, 1998).

6. "Development Affecting Rivers and Wetlands Boomerangs to Cause Economic and Biological Loss," Worldwatch Institute press release, March, 23, 1998, <http://www.worldwatch.org/alerts/pr960323.html> (August 21, 1998).

7. Ibid.

8. Neelam Mathews, "Dying Oceans Are Studied by New Independent Group," *The Earth Times*, December 28, 1997, <http://www.earthtimes.org/dec/waterresouces dyingoceansdec28_97.htm> (March 16, 1998).

9. "Development Affecting Rivers."

10. "Is the Clean Water Act Protecting U.S. Beaches?" *Science and the Environment*, September 1996, <http://www.cais.com/publish/stories/0996mar8.htm> (September 1, 1998).

11. Livernash

12. Douglas H. Chadwick and Joel Sartore, *The Company We Keep: America's Endangered Species* (Washington: National Geographic Society, 1996), p 47.

13. C. Gerald Fraser, "Industries Draining Global Water Resources More than Ever," *The Earth Times*, May 7, 1998, <http://www.earthtimes.org/may/environmentindustriesdrainingmay7_98.htm> (August 16, 1998).

14. Mathews, "Dying Oceans Are Studied by New Independent Group."

Chapter Seven. The Shrinking Land Beneath Our Feet

1. "What Are Wetlands," *United States Environmental Protection Agency*, n.d., <http://www.epa.gov/OWOW/wetlands/vital/what.html> (December 7, 1999).

2. Christina G. Miller and Louise A. Berry, *Jungle Rescue: Saving the New World Tropical Rain Forests* (New York: Simon and Schuster, 1991), pp. 75–76.

3. Miller, pp. 70–74.

4. "Biodiversity," Biodiversity Resource Center, California Academy of Sciences, n.d., <http://www.calacademy.org/research/library/biodiv.htm> (April 10, 1998).

5. Miller, pp. 70, 85.

6. Ibid., pp. 68–69.

7. "U.S. Leads World Meat Stampede," Worldwatch Institute press release, July 4, 1998, <http://www.

worldwatch.org/alerts/pr980704.html> (August 21, 1998).

8. "What Are Wetlands?"

9. Marshall Taylor, "Wetland Mitigation Banks Strike Balance Between Development and Restoration," *Real Estate Finance Today*, July 15, 1996, <http://www.cais.net/publish/stories/0996bio8.htm> (March 16, 1998).

10. "Report Calls for Rapid Scaling Up of Efforts to Preserve Health of Forests and Provide Economic Benefits," Worldwatch Institute press release, April 4, 1998, <http://www.worldwatch.org/alerts/pr980402.html> (August 21, 1998).

11. "Wild Lands for Wildlife," *United States Fish and Wildlife Service*, n.d., <http://www.refuges.fws.gov/NWRSFiles/General/wildlands.html> (September 1, 1998).

12. Ibid.

13. Neelam Mathews, "Travel Industry Is Busily Putting on a Green Face," *The Earth Times*, December 23, 1997, <http://www.earthtimes.org/dec/ecotravelindustrydec23_97.htm> (March 16, 1998).

14. Michel Batisse, "Biosphere Reserves," *Environment*, June 1997, pp. 12, 14, 15.

15. "Waste Management," *Environmental Trust Fund*, n.d., <http://www.biffa_hti.org.uk/waste/wm_index.html> (September 1, 1998).

16. "Polluting the Earth," *World Book*, 1998, <http://www.worldbook.com/fun/wbla/earth/html/ed07.htm> (August 6, 1998).

17. "Recycling Organic Waste: A Win-Win Proposition," Worldwatch Institute press release, August 2, 1997, <http://www.worldwatch.org/alerts/pr970802.html> (August 21, 1998).

Chapter Eight. Biodiversity Enriches Our Earth

1. Douglas H. Chadwick and Joel Sartore, *The Company We Keep: America's Endangered Species* (Washington: National Geographic Society, 1996).

2. "Damage to Nature Now Causing Widespread 'Natural' Disasters, Economic Hardship," Worldwatch Institute press release, February 11, 1997, <http://www.worldwatch.org/alerts/pr970211.html> (December 7, 1999).

3. "Biodiversity," *Green Generation*, n.d., <http://www.aber.ac.uk/grewww/whatbiodiv.html> (April 10, 1998).

4. Hatsy Shields, "Converted at Cullowhee," *House Beautiful*, July 1997, pp. 35–36.

5. Maha Aziz, "Activists Blame Mexican Salt Plant for Deaths of Endangered Sea Turtles," *The Earth Times*, July 16, 1998, <http://www.earthtimes.org/jul/environmentactivistsblamejul16_98.htm> (August 16, 1998).

6. "Life Without Elders," *San Diego Zoo*, March 10, 1998, <http://www.sandiegozoo.org/pressbox/> (December 7, 1999); Traci Watson, "Reptile Smugglers Snared, U.S. Says," *USA Today*, September 16, 1998, p. 3A.

7. Brenda Biondo, "Born to Be Wild," *USA Weekend*, August 21–23, 1998, p. 8.

8. Ibid.

9. Paul Spencer Sochaczewski, "New-Breed Conservationists Save Nature by Applying Sound Business Principles," *The Earth Times*, February 5, 1998, <http://www.earthtimes.org/feb/environmentnewbreedfeb5_98.htm> (March 16, 1998).

10. Ibid.

11. "How Can Kids Help?" *United States Fish and Wildlife Service*, n.d., <http://www.fws.gov/kids/how_help.htm> (April 1, 2000).

Further Reading

Andryszewski, Tricia. *The Environment and the Economy: Planting the Seeds for Tomorrow's Growth*. Brookfield, Conn.: Millbrook Press Inc., 1995.

Dashefsky, H. Steven. *Kids Can Make a Difference! Environmental Science Activities*. New York: McGraw, 1995.

Earthworks Group. *50 Simple Things Kids Can Do to Save the Earth*. Kansas City: Andrews & McNeel, 1990.

Gardner, Robert. *Celebrating Earth Day: A Sourcebook of Activities and Experiments*. Brookfield, Conn.: Millbrook Press Inc., 1992.

Gartner, Robert. *Working Together Against the Destruction of the Environment*. New York: Rosen Group, 1994.

Holmes, Anita. *I Can Save the Earth: A Kid's Handbook for Keeping Earth Healthy and Green*. N.J.: Silver Burdett, 1993.

Landau, Elaine. *Environmental Group: The Earth Savers*. N.J.: Enslow, 1993.

Miles, Betty. *Save the Earth: An Action Handbook for Kids*. New York: Alfred A. Knopf, 1991.

Miller, Christina G., and Louise A. Berry. *Jungle Rescue: Saving the New World Tropical Rain Forests*. New York: Athenaeum, 1991.

Netzley, Patricia D. *Issues in the Environment*. Calif.: Lucent Books, 1997.

Internet Resources

<http://www.kidsface.org>

The homepage of an environmental group started and run by children.

<http://www.smokeybear.com>

Remember, only you can prevent forest fires.

<http://www.amnh.org/science/biodiversity/>

A great Web site with online activities on biodiversity from the American Museum of Natural History in New York.

<http://www.astc.org/exhibitions/rotten/rthome.htm>

This online exhibition takes an in-depth look at the complex issues surrounding garbage and recycling; many activities.

<http://www.enviroweb.org/edf/>

This site offers an online exhibit with games and plenty of information on global warming.

<http://seawifs.gsfc.nasa.gov/ocean_planet.html>

"Ocean Planet" is an online exhibit from the Smithsonian Institution.

<http://www.nwf.org/kids/>

National Wildlife Federation Web site for kids with games, activities, and Ranger Rick.

<http://www.ran.org/ran/kids_action/index.html>

Rainforest Action Network's page for kids.

<http://www.dnr.state.wi.us/org/caer/ce/eek/index.htm>
An electronic magazine on the environment for children grades 4–8.

<http://www.kidsplanet.org/>
Interactive wildlife and conservation site featuring games, quizzes, fact sheets, stories, teacher resources, and great activities.

<http://www.energy.ca.gov/education/index.html>
Energy education for kids from the California Energy Commission.

<http://www.rainforest-alliance.org/kids&teachers/index.html>
Activities and information for kids about preserving rain forests. Also has a list of other environmental Web sites for children.

<http://ecokids.earthday.ca/>
A Canadian Web site with Earth Day and environmental activities for children.

<http://www.audubon.org/educate/>
Virtual tours, activities, and information from a well-known bird conservation organization.

<http://www.wilderness.org/kidscorner/index.htm>
Wilderness Society's Kid's Corner with an online coloring book, quizzes, and information.

<http://www.ssc.org/>
Web site of the Sierra Student Coalition, affiliated with the Sierra Club.

<http://www.eelink.net/studentenvironmentaleducationsites.html>
A list of environmental Web links for children.

<http://www.cochran.com/theodore/beritsbest/>

This Web site has a great list of links on many subjects, including "environment" and "Earth Day." All links are appropriate for children, have descriptions, and are rated.

<http://www.epa.gov/kids/>

The EPA hosts a number of very good Web sites for children with games, activities, and information.

<http://www.epa.gov/superfund/kids/>

A separate Web site from the EPA that introduces the important work of the Superfund program to children with more games and activities.

Index